SHOW-ME-HOW
I Can Cook

How-to-cook activity projects for the very young

SARAH MAXWELL

LORENZ BOOKS

LONDON • NEW YORK • SYDNEY • BATH

This book is dedicated with love and thanks
to Paul, Oliver and Jenny.

First published in 1995 by Lorenz Books
an imprint of Anness Publishing Limited
1 Boundary Row
London SE1 8HP

© Anness Publishing Limited 1995

Reprinted in 1996

This edition published in Australia in 1995
by Koala Book Company, 722 Bourke Street
Redfern, N.S.W. 2016, Australia

ISBN 1 85967 067 9

A CIP catalogue record of this book
is available from the British Library.

Editorial Director: Joanna Lorenz
Project Editors: Judith Simons and Emma Wish
Designer: Edward Kinsey
Photographer: John Freeman
Home Economist and Stylist: Sarah Maxwell
Printed and bound in China

PLEASE NOTE
**All the recipes in this book have been created with
simplicity, effectiveness and fun in mind.
However, there are some stages in the recipes
where potentially dangerous utensils or
equipment are needed. The level of adult
supervision will depend on the ability and age of
the child, but we advise that adult supervision is
always preferable and vital if the project calls for
the use of sharp knives or other utensils. Never
leave a child cooking alone in the kitchen and
always take total charge over the oven, grill or
stove top.**

ACKNOWLEDGEMENTS
The publishers would like to thank the following
children for appearing in this book, and of course
their parents: Alexandra and Oliver Hall, George
Wheeler, Karina Kelly, Tania and Joshua Ayshford,
Andreas Wiseman, Sophie, Alex and Otis
Lindblom-Smith, Tania Murphy.

Contents

Introduction

This book is full of great ideas and recipes for you to create in your kitchen. Some of the recipes are quite simple to follow. Others will require a bit more concentration for you to get them absolutely right. A few allow you to really get your hands in and get as mucky as you like. There are recipes for starters and snacks, main meals and lots of ideas for special occasion treats that will really impress your friends. But remember, whether easy or difficult, all the ideas here have been specially designed for you to get lots of fun, pleasure and compliments from your cooking.

One thing is certain, by the time you have tried all the recipes in this book you will be an expert cook. Family and friends will be forever inviting themselves over to sample your famous cooking.

Whatever you are going to make, there are always a few very important rules to remember before you start. Be safe, be clean and be patient as recipes can easily turn into disasters if you try to rush things or cut corners to save time.

Peel potatoes with a vegetable peeler.

Always read through the recipe you are planning to make. Write out a list of what you need, but before you go shopping, check the cupboards to see if there are any ingredients you already have, so won't have to buy. It is also a good idea to make a note of how much of a particular ingredient you need, as this will stop you from buying too much and spending too much money. Ask a grown-up to have a quick look through your list before you set off, and always take a grown-up or big brother or sister with you when you go to the shops.

While you are cooking, there will be some stages when it will be useful to have a grown-up close by. More importantly, always ask a grown-up to help with potentially dangerous jobs like transferring food in and out of the oven and on and off the stove top. You will also need help from a grown-up with any stages in the recipe for which you need sharp knives, scissors or electrical equipment, and when anything hot is being handled. Make sure in advance that a grown-up is going to be available if you need them and always get

Always ask a grown-up to hold hot saucepans for you.

Garnish the finished dish to make it look more appetizing.

permission from a grown-up before you start creating your chosen dish in the kitchen.

The recipes in this book show you, in detailed stages, what you should be doing at each step of the cooking. Just take a look at the children in the pictures and follow what they are doing.

So, when you have read through the rest of the information in the introduction, off you go.

Good luck and have fun!

First Things First

You've chosen your recipe and bought your ingredients, but there are a few simple things to do before you actually start to cook. If there is anything you don't understand, ask a grown-up to explain it to you.

❖ Read through the recipe, from start to finish, very carefully so you have a clear idea of what you are about to be doing and in what order.

❖ Wash and dry your hands. If your hair is long, tie it back. Put on an apron to protect your clothes – plastic ones are best.

❖ Make sure the kitchen surfaces are clean and tidy and you have plenty of space in which to work.

❖ Get all the ingredients you will need sorted out and weighed.

Biscuit cutters come in all different shapes and sizes and are great for making biscuits or cutting out fun sandwich shapes.

Weighing and Measuring

The ingredients in this book are measured in grams (g) and millilitres (ml), known as metric measures, and also in ounces (oz) and pints (pt), known as imperial measures. You will also see tsp for teaspoon and tbsp for tablespoon (you might be able to get a

set of special measuring spoons to help you weigh these small amounts).

It is very important that you choose *either* metric *or* imperial measures when you are weighing out your ingredients. Never mix the two units – use either grams or ounces, not a combination.

If you want to cook a particular recipe in this book, but you want to make it for more or less people, you can increase or reduce the quantities of ingredients to suit you. If you need help with the multiplication or division, ask a grown-up to help you out.

Why Things Go Wrong

If you find that things are not turning out as they should, then make sure you are following this list of handy tips.

❖ Don't rush.

❖ Do read the recipe through before you start, and follow the instructions and pictures closely.

❖ Do weigh and measure the ingredients carefully.

❖ Don't have any interruptions or distractions while you are in the kitchen, as this can cause you to forget where you are in the recipe, and leave bits out.

❖ If cooking in the oven, don't keep opening the oven door as this will cause the temperature to drop.

❖ Do make sure you cook things for the proper length of time.

A food processor makes mixing ingredients easy and quick. Always ask a grown-up to help you with this piece of equipment.

To cook successfully, you must always weigh your ingredients carefully.

Be Clean and Tidy

When you are cooking and handling food, you must be aware of the bacteria which are all around. Most bacteria are harmless, but it is important to keep the harmful ones away by following a few simple rules.

❖ Always wash your hands before you handle food and keep washing them every now and then while you are cooking, to keep them as clean as possible.

❖ Wear a clean apron and tie long hair back.

❖ Have a clean, damp cloth handy, so you can wipe the surfaces if you make a mess. Don't forget to rinse the cloth when you have used it.

Wash your hands before you start to cook and dry them on a clean dish towel.

❖ Try to tidy up and wash up as you go, so you won't have so much to do at the end.

❖ Wash your chopping board regularly and every time you use it for a new ingredient.

❖ Always wash fruit and vegetables before you use them and clear away any peelings.

❖ Have a rubbish bin near by, so you can keep putting things in it rather than letting the rubbish pile up as you cook.

Be Safe in the Kitchen

There are some things in the kitchen which can be very dangerous. Make sure you have a grown-up's permission before you start cooking and ask them to be around to help with the more dangerous stages of cooking. Always read through the recipe to see when and where you might need the help of a grown-up, then follow these basic rules:

❖ Always ask a grown-up to light the oven or stove top – never do it yourself.

❖ Go slowly and carefully in the kitchen – rushing around causes accidents.

❖ Always use oven gloves or a dish towel when handling hot things. Better still, ask a grown-up to do it for you.

❖ Never leave the kitchen when something is cooking – you don't know what might happen while you're gone!

Always wear an apron to protect your clothes when cooking.

Place hot bowls or saucepans on a trivet to protect the work surface, and use oven gloves or a dish towel to hold hot things.

❖ Make sure you turn saucepan or frying pan handles to the sides of the cooker when they're on the stove top. This will stop you knocking or catching yourself on them.

❖ Never touch electrical equipment, plugs, sockets or switches when your hands are wet. You might get an electric shock.

❖ Take great care when using sharp knives. Chop on a chopping board and point the knife downwards. Keep all your fingers well out of the way.

❖ Stand away from frying food or boiling water. Always ask a grown-up to do these stages for you.

❖ If you spill anything on the floor while you are cooking, wipe it up straight away, otherwise you might forget it's there and have a nasty accident later.

❖ It's a good idea to have a heatproof mat or trivet handy on the table to put hot pans straight on to.

Always use a chopping board when cutting things and keep your fingers away from the knife.

Preparing Vegetables

Most vegetables need washing and peeling before you can use them in your recipes. Some need chopping or slicing. It might be safer to get a grown-up to do this for you. If you can do it yourself, here are some common vegetables and ways to prepare them for use.

Slicing and chopping an onion To slice the onion in half, put the flat side on the chopping board and slice across the onion from side to side. If you want to chop it, try to keep the slices together and slice down from the top to the bottom.

Cut an onion in half, peel off the skin and then slice or chop it carefully with a sharp knife.

Shredding carrot Grate a carrot through the biggest holes on the grater. Or, with the help of a grown-up, you can do it in the food processor.

Shredding lettuce Use a crunchy lettuce such as an Iceberg. Remove the outer leaves and then cut the lettuce in half from the top to the bottom. Lay the flat side on your chopping board and cut across at about 12 mm ($^1/_2$ in) intervals. This will give you ribbon strips of varying lengths.

Cucumber slices and strips Cut a length from the cucumber and peel it with a vegetable peeler if you like. Cut it in half lengthways. Put the flat side on your board. For slices, cut across the half as finely as you can. For strips, cut the cucumber half lengthways into three thick slices and then cut each slice from top to bottom into long strips.

Peel carrots with a vegetable peeler before you grate them.

Glossary

Here are some cookery words and their meanings that are used in the recipes. These will help to make things clearer when you are following the instructions.

Beat Mix ingredients together very hard, stirring with a wooden spoon.

Boil Cook at a high heat on the stove top until the water or food bubbles fast.

Garnish Add a decoration to savoury food, to make it look more attractive.

Grease Cover baking tins or trays with a light layer of butter, margarine or oil to prevent food sticking to them when it is cooked.

Knead Squeeze, stretch and turn a mixture, usually bread dough, before baking.

Season Add just enough salt and pepper to a recipe to suit your own tastes.

Sift/sieve Shake, tap or press an ingredient through a sieve to remove any lumps and sometimes to add air.

Simmer Cook food over a low heat on the stove top, usually after it has boiled, so that it bubbles gently.

Whisk Beat very hard and fast to add air to a mixture, usually egg whites or cream, until the mixture is light, fluffy and sometimes stiff. This can be done with a hand whisk or an electric mixer.

Things to Have in the Kitchen

Kitchen shops and supermarkets are the best places to go if you want to buy cooking equipment. Here are some of the main things you will need in the kitchen to make the recipes in this book.

Weighing scales

Kitchen roll

Measuring jug

Saucepan

Salt and pepper

Trivet

Sieve

Measuring spoons

Wooden spoons

Hand/balloon whisk

Mixing bowls

Peeler

Knives for chopping and slicing should be sharp. Always have a grown-up nearby when using them. Other knives are useful for spreading or cutting soft things.

Wooden spoons for stirring, beating and mixing ingredients.

A rolling pin comes in handy for rolling pastry and dough.

Cutters and stamps made of metal or plastic are great fun for cutting out biscuits and sandwiches.

Mixing bowls for stirring, beating and mixing ingredients.

Saucepans and a frying pan for cooking on the stove top.

Weighing scales for weighing out ingredients.

A food processor or blender is handy for puréeing ingredients and mixing.

A grater is used for grating cheese and vegetables.

A can opener is used for taking the tops off cans.

A hand/balloon whisk is necessary for whisking air into things like eggs and cream.

A palette knife is ideal for spreading soft things, such as icing, and flipping pancakes.

A measuring jug is used for measuring liquid ingredients, such as milk and water.

A chopping board is needed for chopping and slicing things on. It is more hygienic than working directly on to the work surface or table top.

Measuring spoons are needed for measuring small amounts of ingredients, wet and dry. Most useful are 15 ml (1 tbsp) and 5 ml (1 tsp).

Sieves are used for getting the lumps out of ingredients.

Dish towels and oven gloves are for holding hot things, and putting dishes into and taking them out of the oven.

A trivet is used for putting hot pans on, as it protects the work surfaces.

A peeler is used for removing the outer layer from vegetables.

Salt and pepper are used to season (add flavour to) food.

Kitchen roll is handy for mopping up spillages, as well as absorbing excess grease from food.

Grater

Oven glove

Food processor

Frying pan

Rolling pin

Dish towels

Cutters and stamps

Palette knife

Knives

Chopping board

9

Egg Bugs and Toadstools

A good thing about this recipe is that you can make the egg bugs and toadstools up to two hours in advance and keep them in the fridge. But don't dot on the mayonnaise. This should be done at the last minute, just before you serve them. Follow what Alexandra is doing and then choose who gets an egg bug and who gets a toadstool.

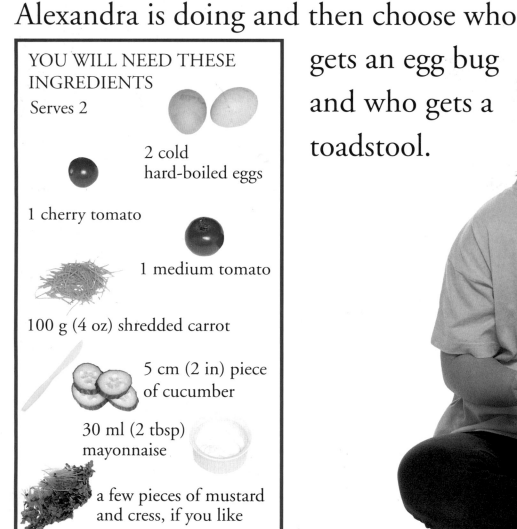

YOU WILL NEED THESE INGREDIENTS

Serves 2

2 cold hard-boiled eggs

1 cherry tomato

1 medium tomato

100 g (4 oz) shredded carrot

5 cm (2 in) piece of cucumber

30 ml (2 tbsp) mayonnaise

a few pieces of mustard and cress, if you like

Special equipment: cocktail stick

Handy hints:
❖ To hard boil the eggs, ask a grown-up to put them in a pan of cold water, bring to the boil and then simmer for about 10 minutes. To cool them down quickly after cooking, drain and return to the saucepan, then place them under cold running water for a few minutes.
❖ Don't bang the eggs too hard when you are trying to crack the shells to peel them. Just tap them gently on the work surface, turning them over as you tap, until the shell is cracked all over. Carefully peel away the shell, without damaging the egg white. It is easier to do this under cold running water.

1 Peel the eggs – see handy hints opposite. Cut a thin slice from the side of one of the eggs, and a slice from the pointed end of the other egg.

2 Cut the cherry tomato in half and then cut one half into four pieces to make the egg bug. Cut the big tomato in half for the toadstool.

3 To make a base on the serving dish, arrange the shredded carrot on a plate, spreading it out so that it is flat and even.

4 Peel away strips of cucumber skin and cut two slices to stand the eggs on. You can cut more for decoration.

5 Place the cucumber slices on top of the shredded carrot, then put an egg on top of each one. Don't forget that the egg bug lies down and the toadstool stands up!

6 To finish off the egg bug, use a cocktail stick to put some mayonnaise on the big end and top of the lying-down egg. Stick on half a cherry tomato for the face and two quarters on top for the spikes. Put a blob of mayonnaise on top of the toadstool egg and put a larger tomato half on top.

7 Use the cocktail stick to put tiny spots of mayonnaise all over the toadstool and to make the eyes, nose and mouth for the egg bug's face. Use mustard and cress for the egg bug's feet.

Cheese Dip with Dunks

This dish that George is making is great for a party and all your friends will love dunking their favourite crisps and vegetables into the rich and creamy dip. Watch out for dunkin' grown-ups, they are bound to want to join in all the fun! If you want to give the strips of vegetables for dunking a crinkled effect, use a crinkle-bladed knife to cut them.

YOU WILL NEED THESE INGREDIENTS
Serves 8–10

225 g (8 oz) carton of full-fat soft cheese

60 ml (4 tbsp) milk

small bunch of fresh chives

1 small carrot, peeled

For dunking: 7.5 cm (3 in) strips of cucumber, 1/2 of a red, orange and yellow pepper, seeded and cut into strips, 4 baby sweetcorn, tortilla chips 8–10 cherry tomatoes

Special equipment: scissors

Handy hints:
❖ If you prefer your dips to be less rich tasting, you could use a low-fat soft cheese instead of full-fat soft cheese.
❖ Chives are a fresh herb which look a little like grass and taste of onions. If you can't find any, you can snip the green tops off spring onions instead.
❖ You could also add celery, cauliflower florets, carrot sticks, slices of apple and radishes to your selection of dipping vegetables.

1 Spoon the full-fat soft cheese into a mixing bowl and beat it with a wooden spoon until soft and creamy.

2 Add the milk to the cheese, a little at a time. Beat the mixture well each time you pour more milk in.

3 Beat the mixture hard for about 2 minutes. If necessary, add more milk to make the dip runnier.

4 Cut the chives finely and add to the cheese mixture, saving some.

5 Grate the carrot on the smallest holes of the greater. Save some and stir the rest into the cheese mixture.

6 Spoon the mixture into a bowl and sprinkle on the remaining chives and grated carrot. Cut the cucumber, baby sweetcorn and peppers for dunking into thin strips.

7 Place the bowl of dip in the centre of a serving plate and arrange little groups of the strips for dunking around the edges. Add the tomatoes and crisps or tortilla chips and let your guests start dippin' and dunkin'.

Sandwich Shapes

You can use any shape cutters you like for these sandwiches, but a selection of different sizes is best because that means less sandwich waste. You can also mix 'n' match the colours of the bread when you make the sandwiches. See how Karina is using a slice of brown bread for the bottom of the sandwich and a slice of white bread for the top.

Handy hints:
❖ To soften the butter or margarine, either leave it out of the fridge for about 30 minutes or microwave it, with the help of a grown-up, on 50% (MEDIUM) for about 15 seconds, or until it is soft.

❖ Use metal biscuit cutters with sharp edges for the best results. Once in position, press down firmly around the edges, making sure you've cut right through to the other side of the sandwich. Remove the cutter and gently press out the cut-out sandwich.

YOU WILL NEED THESE INGREDIENTS
Serves 4–6

8 slices of medium white bread

8 slices of medium brown bread

butter or margarine, for spreading

Ham 'n' cheese filling:
4 thin slices of ham
4 squares of processed cheese

Chicken 'n' mayonnaise filling: 4 thin slices of chicken roll, mayonnaise for spreading

shredded lettuce, radishes, mustard and cress, to garnish

Special equipment: biscuit cutters in different shapes

1 Lay the slices of bread out on the work surface and lightly spread one side with softened butter or margarine.

4 Using your selection of biscuit cutters, stamp out shapes from the sandwiches. Squeeze two or more shapes out of each sandwich if possible.

6 Garnish the plate of sandwiches with a little shredded lettuce, radishes and mustard and cress around the edges. Cover the plate with clear film and keep in the fridge until you're ready to eat the sandwiches.

2 To make the ham 'n' cheese sandwiches, put a slice of ham on four slices of the bread, then put a slice of cheese on top of the ham. For the chicken 'n' mayonnaise sandwiches, put a slice of chicken on four of the remaining slices of bread and spread a little mayonnaise on top.

3 Use the remaining eight slices of bread to make the sandwich lids. Press down lightly on the sandwiches.

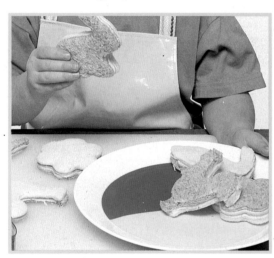

5 Arrange the sandwiches on a serving plate, overlapping them slightly.

Pasta Shapes with Lentil Sauce

Tania is having great fun making this colourful and healthy dish. When you go shopping for the ingredients you need for this recipe, look out for fun pasta shapes, such as animals, vehicles or letters of the alphabet. If you can't find them, any small pasta shapes will do. This is a great recipe for your vegetarian friends because it contains no meat. Check whether the lentils need to be soaked before cooking. If so, follow the instructions on the packet.

Handy hints:
❖ Although the food processor or blender is safe to use once the lid is on properly, it is a good idea to ask a grown-up to help with the tricky stages of inserting and removing the sharp blade.
❖ Another way of serving this recipe is on a large serving platter. Put it in the centre of the table and let everyone help themselves.

YOU WILL NEED THESE INGREDIENTS
Serves 4–6

1 garlic clove, peeled, 1 vegetable stock cube

dash of olive oil

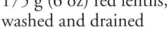

1 onion, peeled and chopped

175 g (6 oz) red lentils, washed and drained

10 ml (2 tsp) tomato purée

575 ml (1 pt) water   pepper

225 g (8 oz) pasta shapes

50 g (2 oz) grated Cheddar cheese

10 ml (2 tsp) chopped, fresh parsley

Special equipment: garlic press, food processor

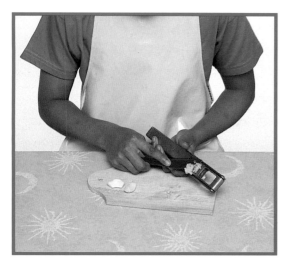

1 Place the garlic clove in the garlic press and squeeze really hard to crush it.

2 Put the crushed garlic in a saucepan. Add the olive oil, chopped onion, lentils and tomato purée. Stir well.

3 Add the water to the saucepan, pouring it over the lentils and other ingredients. Stir again to mix.

4 Crumble the stock cube into the saucepan. Season with pepper, then ask a grown-up to simmer the mixture on the stove top for about 15–20 minutes, until the lentils are cooked.

5 While the lentils are cooking, weigh the pasta shapes. Put the pasta in a saucepan and ask a grown-up to cover it in boiling water, simmer for about 8–10 minutes until tender and drain. Return the pasta to the saucepan, and replace the lid.

6 Ask a grown-up to sieve the hot lentil sauce to remove some of the liquid, leaving a thick, sloppy texture. Put this in a food processor or blender. With the lid of the food processor or blender on tight, press the button to purée the lentil mixture.

7 Ask the grown-up to remove the sharp blade from the food processor or blender. Serve the pasta on to plates and spoon the lentil sauce on top.

Garnish the finished dish with a sprinkling of grated cheese and a little chopped, fresh parsley. Delicious!

17

Funny Face Pizzas

Use your imagination to make your pizzas look happy or sad or just plain silly. Choose your ingredients to suit the expression you want. You can also make up your own hair styles for the pizza faces as Karina has done here, using as much or as little of the mustard and cress as you like. If you don't want a bow tie, then put the kiwi fruit in the hair as a ribbon.

Handy hints:
❖ If you prefer your pizzas slightly flatter, use small round pitta breads instead of burger buns.
❖ If you don't like or can't get mozzarella cheese, use Cheddar cheese instead. It is just as delicious but won't be so 'stringy' when you eat it.

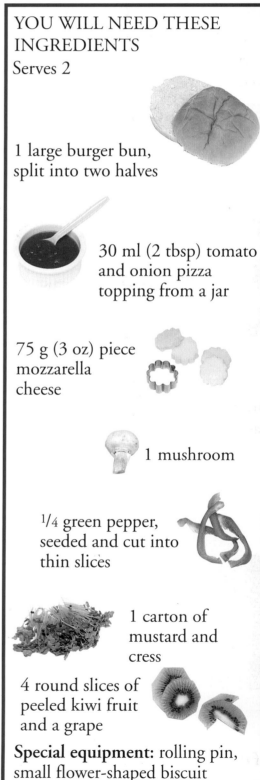

YOU WILL NEED THESE INGREDIENTS
Serves 2

1 large burger bun, split into two halves

30 ml (2 tbsp) tomato and onion pizza topping from a jar

75 g (3 oz) piece mozzarella cheese

1 mushroom

1/4 green pepper, seeded and cut into thin slices

1 carton of mustard and cress

4 round slices of peeled kiwi fruit and a grape

Special equipment: rolling pin, small flower-shaped biscuit cutter

1 Put the bun halves on the work surface. Flatten them gently and evenly all over using the rolling pin.

2 Spread tomato and onion pizza topping over the top of each bun, making sure it goes close to the edges.

3 Cut the piece of mozzarella cheese into thin slices. You could ask a grown-up to do this with a sharp knife.

4 Using the flower-shaped cutter, stamp out four pieces of cheese for the pizzas' eyes. Put two in position on each of the pizza bases and set aside.

5 Wash the mushroom and slice it in half to make two noses. Position the noses on the pizza faces and press down lightly.

6 Use the green pepper slices to make mouths on the faces. Put the pizzas on the grill pan and ask a grown-up to cook them under a hot grill for about 5 minutes, until the cheese has melted a little and the buns are toasted around the edges.

7 Ask the grown-up to put the pizzas on to serving plates. Cut bunches of the mustard with scissors or a knife and put them in neat piles around the top of the faces to look like hair.

Cut the kiwi rounds and grape in half and position them on the plates to make ears and bow ties.

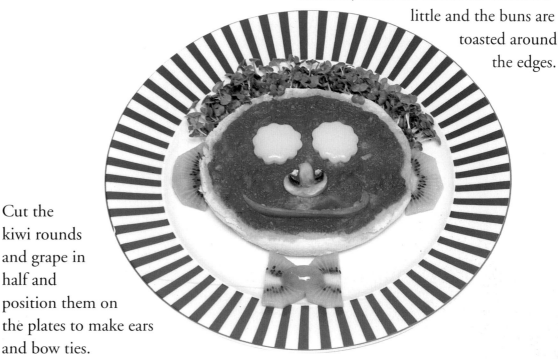

Swimming Fish Cakes

There are lots of variations on this recipe that Joshua is making. You could serve the swimming fish on a sea of your favourite vegetable. Try a sea of peas or sweetcorn, or a mixture of both. If you particularly like modelling, make lots of tiny fish, and serve everyone with two or more. But remember to tell your grown-up helper that the small fish won't take as long to cook as the bigger ones.

Handy hints:
❖ Ask a grown-up to open the can of tuna with a can opener, as this can be dangerous and you might cut yourself.
❖ You could make the fish cake mixture and even shape the cakes up to several hours in advance, if you like. Keep them in the fridge until you are ready to cook and eat them.

YOU WILL NEED THESE INGREDIENTS
Serves 4

25 g (1 oz) butter

3 large potatoes

1 egg   dash of milk

200 g (7 oz) can tuna chunks in brine, drained

75 g (3 oz) fresh breadcrumbs

pepper

oil, for shallow frying

For the garnish:
4 peas

a few sprigs of fresh curly parsley

¹/₂ cucumber peeled, cut in half lengthways and very thinly sliced, 4 slices of lemon, 4 thin slices of tomato

Special equipment: vegetable peeler, potato masher, can opener

1 Peel the potatoes with the peeler, cut into small pieces and put in the saucepan. Cover with water. Ask a grown-up to boil the potatoes for about 15–20 minutes, until soft.

2 Ask a grown-up to drain the potatoes and return them to the saucepan. Place the saucepan on a trivet. Add the butter, milk and egg.

3 Put a dish towel between you and the saucepan to prevent you touching the hot saucepan. Mash the potatoes using the masher until they are smooth, with no lumps.

4 Spoon the mashed potato into a mixing bowl, making sure you scrape it all out of the saucepan. Use a wooden spoon to mix in the tuna, breadcrumbs and pepper. Place the bowl of potato mixture in the fridge to chill for about 30 minutes.

5 Take the bowl out of the fridge and wet your hands slightly. Divide the mixture into four equal portions and, working on a chopping board, mould them into fish shapes.

6 Ask a grown-up to shallow fry the fish cakes in hot oil for about 5 minutes on both sides. Drain the fish cakes on absorbent kitchen paper and transfer to the serving plate.

To garnish your swimming fish, put a pea in position for the eye and a slice of tomato for the mouth of each fish. Use fresh parsley for air bubbles and a lemon slice for the sun in the sky. Arrange the cucumber slices in rows to look like the sea.

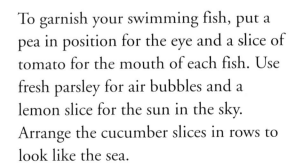

Mini Burgers 'n' Buns

Served with cucumber 'chips', these tasty burgers are easy to make and are ideal for lunch or supper. In this recipe, Oliver has garnished the burgers with lettuce and tomatoes. But if you like your burgers to be filled with lots of salad, then use the lettuce and tomatoes to pack inside your burger roll. You might want a dollop of mayonnaise as well.

Handy hints:

❖ To make fresh breadcrumbs, take a chunk of yesterday's loaf of bread and grate it, up and down, on the coarse grater, just as you would for cheese.

❖ To stop the grill pan from getting greasy while the burgers are cooking, cover the base with a sheet of foil which, when cool, you can screw up and throw away, without having to wash up the pan.

❖ Always use an oven glove or dish towel when you go anywhere near the hot grill or pan. And always remember to ask a grown-up to help, whenever there are hot things around.

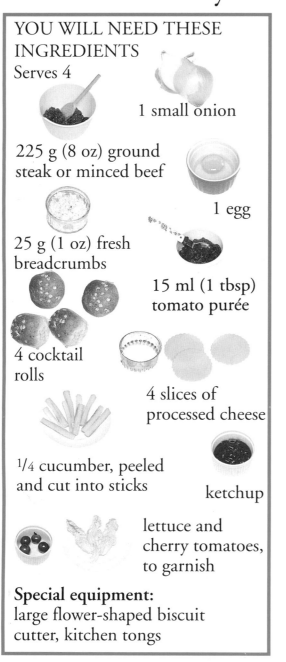

YOU WILL NEED THESE INGREDIENTS

Serves 4

1 small onion

225 g (8 oz) ground steak or minced beef

1 egg

25 g (1 oz) fresh breadcrumbs

15 ml (1 tbsp) tomato purée

4 cocktail rolls

4 slices of processed cheese

¼ cucumber, peeled and cut into sticks

ketchup

lettuce and cherry tomatoes, to garnish

Special equipment: large flower-shaped biscuit cutter, kitchen tongs

1 With help from a grown-up, peel the onion and slice it thinly. Then chop it into tiny pieces.

2 Put the meat in a mixing bowl and add the egg, onion, breadcrumbs and tomato purée.

3 Using a wooden spoon, mix all the ingredients together in the bowl, until they are evenly combined.

4 Wet your hands to stop the burger mixture from sticking to them. Take a small handful of mixture, shape it into a round and flatten it slightly. Do this until all the mixture is used up. Place the burgers on the grill pan.

5 Ask a grown-up to put the burgers under a hot grill for about 5 minutes. Then remove the grill pan – so that you can carefully turn the burgers over with a pair of tongs. Ask the grown-up to put the burgers back under the grill for another 5–8 minutes.

6 Use a knife to carefully cut open the bread rolls on a chopping board. Place the bottom halves of the buns on serving plates.

7 Stamp out the cheese rounds using the cutter and place on the bread roll bottoms. Dollop a little ketchup on top.

Put the burgers on the ketchup and place the bread lids on top. Serve the mini burgers with cucumber 'chips', lettuce and tomatoes for a delicious treat.

Ham and Sweetcorn Roll-ups

With George's delicious recipe any day can be pancake day, so get flipping and tossing. Those with a big appetite can probably eat two roll-ups, otherwise serve one per person. If you and your grown-up helper manage to make them really thin, you might be able to make a few extra to serve sprinkled with sugar and lemon juice or with jam, for a totally pancake meal.

Handy hints:
❖ The frying pan should be very hot before cooking the pancakes, so ask a grown-up to help you.
❖ When you put the rolled pancakes on the baking sheet to heat through in the oven, make sure you space them a little apart. If you don't, they might stick together and break up when you transfer them to the serving plates.
❖ You can, if you prefer, sprinkle the pancakes with cheese and ask a grown-up to melt the cheese under the grill.

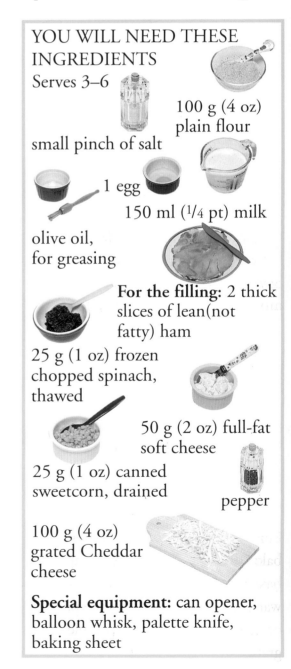

YOU WILL NEED THESE INGREDIENTS
Serves 3–6

small pinch of salt

100 g (4 oz) plain flour

1 egg

150 ml (¹/₄ pt) milk

olive oil, for greasing

For the filling: 2 thick slices of lean(not fatty) ham

25 g (1 oz) frozen chopped spinach, thawed

50 g (2 oz) full-fat soft cheese

25 g (1 oz) canned sweetcorn, drained

pepper

100 g (4 oz) grated Cheddar cheese

Special equipment: can opener, balloon whisk, palette knife, baking sheet

1 Preheat the oven to 200°C/400°F/ Gas 6. Put the flour, salt, milk and egg into a mixing jug. Whisk together until runny and smooth.

2 Ask a grown-up to coat the bottom of a hot, oiled frying pan with the batter. Cook for 1 minute each side and flip with a palette knife.

3 Ask the grown-up to continue making the pancakes. Meanwhile cut the ham into strips and then into squares and put in a mixing bowl.

4 Add the spinach, full-fat soft cheese and sweetcorn to the mixing bowl with the ham. Season the filling mixture with a little pepper, if you like.

5 Stir the filling mixture well, until all the ingredients are mixed in. Lay the pancakes on the work surface.

6 Spoon some of the filling mixture on to each pancake, placing it along the edge nearest you. Roll the pancake around the filling and keep rolling until the filling is completely wrapped up in the pancake.

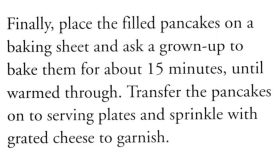

Finally, place the filled pancakes on a baking sheet and ask a grown-up to bake them for about 15 minutes, until warmed through. Transfer the pancakes on to serving plates and sprinkle with grated cheese to garnish.

Colourful Chicken Kebabs

You'll have a great time making your own kebabs and choosing what you put on them. They're brilliant to cook under the grill as Tania is doing here, or on the barbecue with the help of a grown-up. It is best to wash and prepare all the vegetables before you begin threading them on to the skewers. This will help you decide the order of ingredients and stop you getting in a muddle.

Handy hints:
❖ To make your own delicious salad dressing, mix 60 ml (4 tbsp) sunflower oil, 30 ml (2 tbsp) vinegar, 15 ml (1 tbsp) clear honey, and a dash of pepper together in a jar with a tight-fitting lid, then shake it well.
❖ Your grown-up helper may need to add a little more boiling water to the rice while it is cooking, if it looks as if it is drying out before it is cooked.
❖ The reason for soaking the skewers is to prevent them burning during grilling. If they have been soaked in water first, they will not burn so easily.

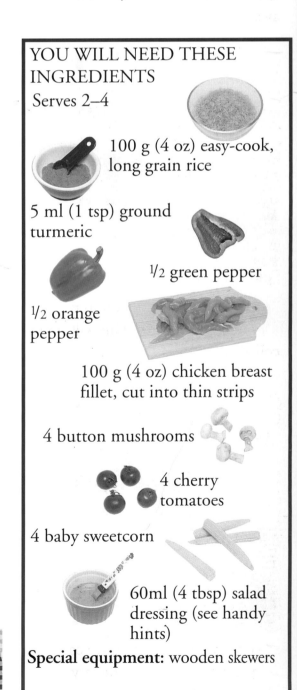

YOU WILL NEED THESE INGREDIENTS
Serves 2–4

100 g (4 oz) easy-cook, long grain rice

5 ml (1 tsp) ground turmeric

½ green pepper

½ orange pepper

100 g (4 oz) chicken breast fillet, cut into thin strips

4 button mushrooms

4 cherry tomatoes

4 baby sweetcorn

60ml (4 tbsp) salad dressing (see handy hints)

Special equipment: wooden skewers

1 Put the wooden skewers in a shallow dish of cold water. Leave them to soak in the water for about 30 minutes, then remove them and throw away the water.

2 Put the rice and turmeric in a saucepan. Ask a grown-up to cover it with boiling water, simmer for 15 minutes, then drain. Return the rice to the saucepan and cover with a lid.

3 While the rice is cooking, put the peppers on a chopping board and cut out the white seeds and pith inside. Rinse the peppers under cold water and cut them into chunks.

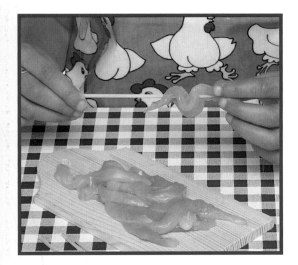

4 Thread the chicken on to the skewers as shown. This will give a coiled effect when it cooks.

5 Thread the other ingredients on to the skewers in whatever order you like. Make sure you finish each one with a piece of baby sweet-corn, pushing the skewer only a little way in.

6 Put the kebabs on the grill pan and drizzle over some of the salad dressing. Ask a grown-up to put the kebabs under a hot grill for about 5 minutes, then to turn them over and continue grilling for another 5 minutes, until the chicken is cooked.

7 Just before the kebabs are cooked, put some rice on to the serving plates and spread it out.

Arrange the kebabs on the rice and they are ready to serve.

Flowery Quiches

Follow what Tania is doing to see how to get rolling with these fun quiche flowers. The quiches are delicious served hot or cold. If you want to eat them cold, you can make them the day before you need them and keep them in the fridge overnight. Don't add the flowery garnishes until just before you serve them, though, as they could become soggy. If you don't like watercress, use shredded lettuce instead.

Handy hints:

❖ Once you have lined the flan tins with a pastry circle and pressed around the edges, you can trim the rims with a knife, if you like. This will make them look a little neater.

❖ Take care pouring the egg and milk mixture into the quiches. If you use too much, it will overflow.

❖ Use a frozen shortcrust pastry for this recipe, if you like. Remember to let it thaw before using.

YOU WILL NEED THESE INGREDIENTS

Serves 4

a little vegetable oil, for greasing

plain flour, for sprinkling

150 g (5 oz) shortcrust pastry

50 g (2 oz) thinly sliced ham

50 g (2 oz) grated Cheddar cheese

45 ml (3 tbsp) milk

1 egg

pepper

100 g (4 oz) fresh watercress/lettuce

400 g (14 oz) can peach slices drained

Special equipment: 4 individual, fluted flan tins, pastry brush, rolling pin, hand whisk, wire cooling rack

1 Preheat the oven to 200°C/400°F/ Gas 6. To stop the pastry from sticking while cooking, brush the insides of the flan tins with a little vegetable oil using a pastry brush.

2 Sprinkle a little flour on the work surface or board, then use a rolling pin to roll out the pastry thinly. You will need a little flour on the rolling pin, too, to stop it sticking to the pastry.

3 Turn one flan tin upside down on the pastry and with a knife cut a circle around it, slightly bigger than the tin. Do this four times, then press the pastry circles into the tins.

4 Place the ham on a chopping board and slice thinly into small strips. Divide the ham between the pastry cases, spreading it out to fill them.

5 Sprinkle the grated cheese over the top of the ham in each of the flan cases. Spread the cheese out evenly.

6 Put the milk and egg in a mixing jug and beat them together with a hand whisk, until blended. Mix in a little black pepper.

7 Add the egg and milk mixture and ask a grown-up to bake the quiches for 15–20 minutes until the pastry is golden brown and the egg is set.

Ask a grown-up to remove the tins from the oven, leave them to cool on a wire rack and then turn the quiches out of the tins. Put a quiche in the centre of each serving plate and arrange a few peach slices around them. Put the watercress or lettuce around the outsides and in the centres of the quiches.

Crazy Popcorn

This multi-coloured cheesy mixture that Andreas is making will make your party the talk of the town. Have fun choosing your own colours for the popcorn and cheese. If you can't get or don't like Red Leicester or Sage Derby, use yellow Cheddar cheese instead. And if you haven't got a large enough container to hold all of the popcorn, or have a lot of guests who are going to want to eat at once, then fill two containers instead.

Handy hints:
❖ You must use powdered food colouring as liquid colouring will turn the popcorn soggy. You will find the powdered kind in specialist cake decorating shops.
❖ You can buy microwave popcorn which is especially for cooking in the microwave. Follow the instructions on the packet for cooking (ask a grown-up to operate the microwave) and colour it as directed in steps 4–6.

YOU WILL NEED THESE INGREDIENTS
Serves 10–15

15 ml (1 tbsp) vegetable oil

175 g (6 oz) popcorn kernels

green, red and blue powdered food colourings

50 g (2 oz) grated Red Leicester cheese

50 g (2 oz) grated Sage Derby cheese

Special equipment: 3 large plastic bags

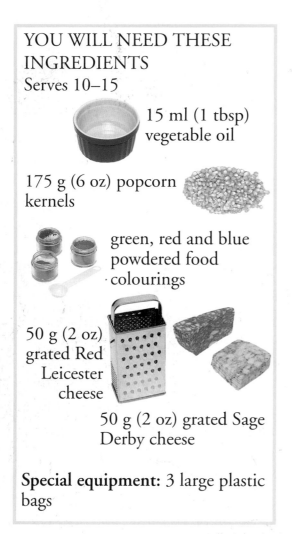

1 Put the vegetable oil in a large saucepan. Pour in the popcorn kernels and stir with a wooden spoon to coat them all in the oil.

2 Place the lid on the saucepan and ask a grown-up to heat the popcorn on the stove top, gently, for about 5 minutes, until you hear the popcorn starting to pop. Do not remove the lid.

3 When the popping noises have slowed down and you hardly hear any popping at all, ask the grown-up to put the saucepan on a trivet on the table. You can now remove the lid.

4 Put small amounts of popcorn in each plastic bag. The bags should be see-through so you can see the colour of the popcorn changing when you add the colour.

5 Use a tiny spoon to add a small amount of food colouring to each of the bags of popcorn. You can choose what colours you use and how much popcorn you want to make a particular colour.

6 Close the bag and hold it tightly in one hand. Shake the bag and tap it with the other hand, tossing the popcorn inside the bag to coat it evenly in the colouring. As you colour each batch, tip it into a large bowl.

7 When all the popcorn is coloured, add the grated cheese.

Wash your hands, then carefully toss the mixture together evenly. Try not to tip it over the sides of the container.

Frozen Banana Lollies

Handy hints:
❖ You can buy lolly sticks in most hardware shops and supermarkets, but if you want to be crafty and environmentally friendly collect up your own and your friends' used ones. Wash and dry them and they'll be as good as new!
❖ Don't peel the bananas too early, otherwise they will start to go brown and mushy.

These lollies are great for a summer party. But if you haven't got any party plans, just make a batch of lollies and freeze them all for yourself. They will keep in the freezer, in sealed bags, for about a month. Sophie has coated her lollies with coconut, but if you don't like it, choose your own coating. Try toasted, chopped nuts or crumbled chocolate flake bars. They are all delicious!

YOU WILL NEED THESE INGREDIENTS
Serves 8

red, blue and green food colourings (powdered or liquid)

100 g (4 oz) desiccated coconut

8 small bananas

a little maple syrup

Special equipment: 8 lolly sticks, pastry brush, baking sheet, clear film

1 Divide the coconut into three small bowls and add a small amount of food colouring to each. Stir well, until the coconut is evenly coloured.

2 Pour the red, blue and green coloured coconut on to separate plates and spread it out evenly.

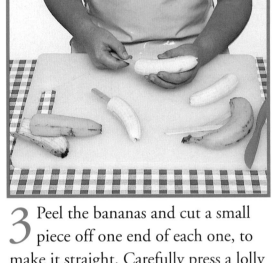

3 Peel the bananas and cut a small piece off one end of each one, to make it straight. Carefully press a lolly stick into the straight end of each banana, taking care not to push the stick in too far, as it might break through the side.

4 Pour some maple syrup into a bowl. Holding the lolly stick and using a pastry brush, brush an even coating of maple syrup over each banana. Put on a plate when coated.

5 Still holding the lolly sticks, dip and roll the bananas in the coloured coconut until they are coated evenly.

6 Lay the bananas on a baking sheet covered with clear film. The bananas must not touch. Freeze for 4 hours.

Take the banana lollies off the baking sheet and arrange on a serving plate. Ideally you should wait about 15 minutes, to let the bananas soften a little before you eat them.

Marshmallow Dip Sticks

These are a lot of fun to make on a rainy day. You'll find they will really cheer you up! Andreas is using different-sized and also different-coloured marshmallows. Check what is available at the supermarket, you might be able to get green ones as well as the usual pink and white. Also, look out for chocolate sugar strands or little silver balls, sometimes called dragees, to use for decoration.

Handy hints:
❖ An alternative way to melt the chocolate is in the microwave. Ask a grown-up to put the broken pieces in a microwave bowl and microwave at 50% (MEDIUM) for about 3–4 minutes, stirring every minute. If you do it this way, the bowl won't heat up and it will be easier for you to handle. Otherwise you must wear oven gloves or use a dish towel.

YOU WILL NEED THESE INGREDIENTS

Serves 8

16 marshmallows

175 g (6 oz) plain dessert chocolate

50 g (2 oz) multi-coloured sugar strands (hundreds and thousands)

Special equipment: scissors, 8 drinking straws

1 Arrange the marshmallows neatly on a chopping board and set on one side.

2 Break the chocolate up into a bowl. Ask a grown-up to put the bowl over a saucepan of simmering water until the chocolate melts.

3 Ask the grown-up to put the hot bowl on a trivet. Hold the bowl with a dish towel and stir the chocolate to make sure it is all melted.

4 Cut about eight coloured straws in half using the scissors. Thin straws are best for this as they push into the marshmallows more easily.

5 Hold a straw in one hand and a marshmallow in the other. Press and turn the straw into the centre of the marshmallow until it is secure.

6 Dip each marshmallow halfway into the melted chocolate. Turn and scrape off any excess chocolate on to the side of the bowl.

7 When the marshmallow is coated in chocolate, dip it straight into the coloured sugar strands, rolling and turning it, until it is evenly coated.

Arrange the finished marshmallows on a serving plate, making sure they do not touch. Leave for about 1 hour, then dive in!

Cut-out Cookies

Any cutter, any shape and any size is good for this recipe. You can also use chocolate sugar strands or flaked chocolate, or even chopped, coloured glacé cherries as decoration. Whatever you choose, be sure to make lots as Alex is doing, because these yummy biscuits will certainly get eaten up very quickly. It's a good idea to have a second baking sheet and a second serving plate handy!

Handy hints:

❖ To save your energy, ask a grown-up to help you use an electric hand mixer to make the dough, or you could make it in a food processor.

❖ When you have cut out the first lot of biscuits from the rolled out dough, gather up all the trimmings and roll them out again. Now you can cut out another lot of biscuits. Keep doing this until all the biscuit dough is used up.

❖ Before you start to drizzle the icing over the biscuits, put a big sheet of greaseproof paper under the wire rack. This will catch all the drips of icing and when you are finished, you just gather up the paper and throw it away.

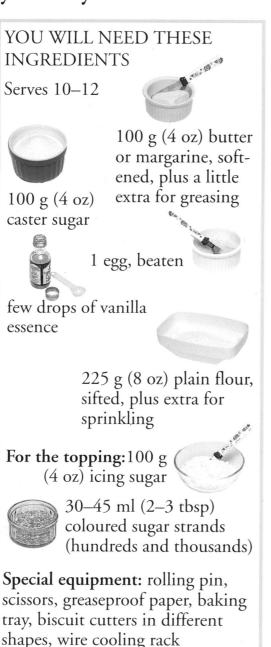

YOU WILL NEED THESE INGREDIENTS

Serves 10–12

100 g (4 oz) caster sugar

100 g (4 oz) butter or margarine, softened, plus a little extra for greasing

1 egg, beaten

few drops of vanilla essence

225 g (8 oz) plain flour, sifted, plus extra for sprinkling

For the topping: 100 g (4 oz) icing sugar

30–45 ml (2–3 tbsp) coloured sugar strands (hundreds and thousands)

Special equipment: rolling pin, scissors, greaseproof paper, baking tray, biscuit cutters in different shapes, wire cooling rack

1 Preheat the oven to 200°C/400°F/ Gas 6. Put the butter and sugar in a mixing bowl and beat with a wooden spoon, until light and fluffy.

2 Add the egg and a few drops of vanilla essence and keep beating until the mixture is smooth.

3 Carefully stir in the flour, mixing well, until a stiff dough starts to form in the bowl.

4 Flour the board and your hands and knead the dough until smooth. Sprinkle more flour and roll out the dough until quite thin. Keep your rolling pin well floured to stop it sticking to the dough.

5 Put a greased sheet of greaseproof paper on to a greased baking tray. Using the cutters, cut out the biscuit shapes and place them on the baking tray. Ask a grown-up to bake the biscuits for 10 minutes.

6 Ask a grown-up to put the biscuits on a wire rack to cool. Put the icing sugar in a bowl and stir in about 15 ml (1 tbsp) of cold water. Mix well.

7 Use a teaspoon to drizzle the icing over the biscuits.

Sprinkle the coloured sugar strands over the biscuits, to decorate. Put the finished biscuits on a plate. Do not pile them up or they will stick. Leave the biscuits for about 30 minutes to let the icing set, then serve.

Cake-cream Cones

Handy hints:
❖ Make sure you don't press the cakes too firmly into the cones, otherwise the cones might break.
❖ Use separate knives for the different icing colours, otherwise you'll mix the colours and they will look messy.
❖The cake-cream cones can be made up to 3 hours in advance and kept in the fridge.

These cones that Alex, Sophie and Otis are eating will fool everybody. If you put them on the table with lots of decorations around them, all your guests will think they're real ice-cream.

YOU WILL NEED THESE INGREDIENTS

Serves 3

100 g (4 oz) fondant moulding icing

175 g (6 oz) icing sugar

75 g (3 oz) butter or margarine, softened

30–45 ml (2–3 tbsp) milk

green and pink food colourings, 10 ml (2 tsp) cocoa

3 small fairy cakes

coloured sugar strands, chocolate sugar strands

3 ice-cream cones

chocolate flake bars and wafers, to decorate

Special equipment: egg boxes (one large or two small), foil, pencil

1 To make holders for the cones, turn the egg boxes upside-down. Press the fondant icing into the hollows, shaping a hole to support the bottom of the cones.

2 Cover the boxes in foil, making sure the joins are underneath. Place on the work surface, with the filled hollows on top. Feel the hollows, then pierce the foil with a pencil.

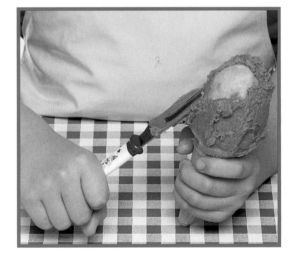

3 To make butter icing, put the icing sugar in a mixing bowl with the butter or margarine and the milk. Use a wooden spoon to mix the icing until it is smooth and creamy.

4 Divide the butter icing into three bowls. Add a speck of food colouring to two bowls and the cocoa to the third. Mix until evenly coloured.

5 Remove any paper from the bottom of the fairy cakes. Gently press a cake into the top of a cone, twisting it slightly until it stays in. Repeat with the other cakes and cones.

6 Spread the icing on to the cake, working from the top downwards. Put the cone in the stand to hold it safely while you coat the rest.

7 Sprinkle with sugar strands, and lightly press chocolate flake bars and wafers into the cakes.

Jelly Pond

By moulding fondant icing just like play-dough, you can be really creative with this recipe and make your own monsters for a lake or pond scene. Follow what Sophie is doing to see how. Try water snakes, ducks, waterlilies, fish and frogs. Your lake or pond will be even more realistic if you add a spot of green food colouring to the jelly while you are dissolving it.

Handy hints:
❖ It is a good idea to wear rubber gloves when you are colouring the fondant icing, otherwise your hands will get coloured too.
❖ The easiest way to get the colour of the icing even is to roll it out into a sausage shape. Bring the two ends of the sausage together and start rolling out a new sausage. Carry on in this way until you are happy with the colour.
❖ Put the chopped jelly into the 'creature' bowl at the very last minute before serving, as the 'wet' jelly will make the fondant creatures start to leak some of their colour.

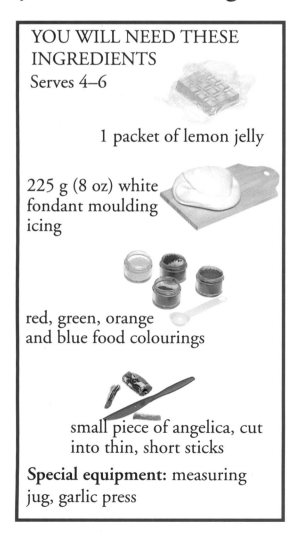

YOU WILL NEED THESE INGREDIENTS
Serves 4–6

1 packet of lemon jelly

225 g (8 oz) white fondant moulding icing

red, green, orange and blue food colourings

small piece of angelica, cut into thin, short sticks

Special equipment: measuring jug, garlic press

1 Break the jelly into small pieces and put it in the mixing jug.

2 With a grown-up, make the jelly according to the packet instructions. Put in the fridge to set.

3 Divide the fondant icing into four portions. Add a speck of food colouring to each, then roll and knead it in.

4 Shape your pond creatures and waterlilies, and press the angelica sticks into a blob of icing for the reeds. Put the shapes for the surface on a plate to dry.

5 To decorate the inside of the jelly bowl, press your underwater creatures to the glass on the inside. Brush a little water on to the creatures' fronts to help them stick better.

6 To make the pond grass, take a small piece of green fondant icing and put it inside a garlic press. Squeeze hard with two hands and watch the grass come out. Use a knife to cut off the grass and put it on a plate to dry and harden.

7 When the jelly is set, use a knife to stir and chop the jelly into tiny pieces. Spoon the jelly into the bowl, taking care not to knock the creatures.

Position all the shapes for the surface of the pond. Make a little scene with the ducks swimming in the pond with the waterlilies and grass all around. Serve immediately.